BEAT PROCRASTINATION FOR GOOD

Change your habits and start getting things done

Written by Hélène Nguyen Gateff

Translated by Rebecca Neal

50MINUTES.com
PROPEL
YOUR BUSINESS FORWARD!
NETWORKING
Effective CV Writing
Resolving Office Conflict
Boost Your Concentration
Find Your Work-Life Balance
www.50minutes.com

BEAT PROCRASTINATION FOR GOOD

- **Problem:** how can I stop constantly delaying all the tasks that I want to complete but, for one reason or another, keep putting off?
- **Uses:** when we stop avoiding the things we need to do and finally become efficient at work and at home, we are rewarded with a feeling of calm and well-deserved peace of mind.
- **Professional context:** personal organisation at work, project management, etc.
- **FAQs:**
  - What exactly does the term 'procrastination' mean?
  - Is there a standard profile of a procrastinator?
  - Does modern life encourage procrastination?
  - What are the potential causes of procrastination?
  - There must be some benefits to procrastination. What are they?
  - What tasks encourage procrastination?
  - How long will it take me to change my behaviour?
  - I cannot manage to overcome my procrastination alone. How can I get help?

"What do you feel when you think about your tendency to put things off until tomorrow?" This question was asked to people of varying ages who had admitted to this behaviour. They all explained that procrastination inspired negative emotions:

- a feeling of guilt: "I know I shouldn't", "I never feel

relaxed";
- a feeling of loss of control: "I can't help it, I'm overwhelmed";
- low self-esteem: "I can't deal with it", "I'm running away from my problems", "I don't have enough willpower".

Real procrastination, the kind that leaves you with a to-do list that gets longer every day, will sooner or later have an impact on your professional and personal life.

Do you see yourself as a regular or occasional procrastinator, whether in your professional life or your personal life? Do you want to finally stop putting off the same tasks? This desire to change is the most important thing, because you will not find the will to break this habit unless you truly want to.

Follow our three-step plan to change your behaviour. Thanks to a few techniques and tricks, you will stop putting off until tomorrow what you can do today.

PUTTING PROCRASTINATION BEHIND YOU: THE BASICS

At this stage, all you have to do is define your goals. To do this, you will need to draw up four lists. Spend no more than 30 minutes on this exercise.

Your unsorted list of tasks

Make a list, in no particular order, of the things you would like to do, but continually put off. Include both personal and professional tasks, without worrying about how important they are. For example:

- file the bills from the last six months,
- sew the button back on my coat,
- organise a regional meeting,
- update my CV,
- telephone five potential new clients,
- prepare my sales presentation, set for ten days from now,
- clear out and tidy my cellar,
- change the tyre on my bike,
- fix my bookshelves,
- make a doctor's appointment.

As you can see, this type of list includes both large tasks with major consequences and minor tasks which have relatively little impact. The important thing is not to try to put them in any kind of order; just jot down anything that comes to mind without beating yourself up about it.

Your list of inconveniences

Next, select the ten tasks that you consider most important (if you have fewer than ten to start with, even better!) and quickly analyse the inconveniences that come with putting them off. Thinking about these negative effects and writing them down will help you to identify sources of motivation and establish your priorities. You should describe the inconveniences very precisely, as in the table below.

Task put off	Inconveniences linked to putting off
File the bills from the last six months	• I waste time every time I look for a bill. • My manager thinks I am unserious and disorganised.
Change the punctured tyre on my bike	• I am frustrated because I cannot use my bike. • I am tired and irritated due to a lack of exercise.
Sew the button back on my coat	• I am annoyed every morning when I look in the mirror and see the missing button. • I think I look untidy.
Update my CV	• I feel that I am not taking control of changing my job and that I am getting trapped in a situation that is not good for me.

Your list of benefits

Transform this table by picturing your situation once you have completed the ten tasks. Think "Once I have finished this task, I will get the following benefit from it" rather than

"If I finished this task, I would get the following benefit from it". This simple rewording exercise will allow you to change your attitude.

Task	Benefit
Once I have filed the bills from the last six months...	• ...I will not waste any more time looking for them, and I will be able to use the time saved for a rewarding activity (a coffee, a break). • ...my manager will have a more positive view of me.
Once I have changed the punctured tyre on my bike...	• ...I will be able to go out into the woods with my friends on Sundays, get some fresh air and relax.
Once I have sewn the button back on my coat...	• ...I will think that I look tidier when I look in the mirror.
Once I have updated my CV...	• ...I will have reviewed the kind of job I can aspire to, I will be more easily able to envisage myself in the future, and I will be ready to respond to a potential job posting.

Your list of distractions

Now think about the things in your environment that encourage your tendency to put things off until tomorrow and pick four elements that you can act on. Next, decide to do something to eliminate each distraction. For example:

Distraction	Action
I do not sleep enough because I watch television until late at night.	I will move the television so that I am no longer tempted to watch it in bed.
I do not have enough energy in the mornings because I get up too late to have time for breakfast.	I will set my alarm for 15 minutes earlier and take the time to make myself breakfast. As I am slow in the mornings, I will set the table the night before.
I often have lunch with colleagues who talk negatively.	I will have lunch earlier or later, using a diet or shopping as an excuse.
I check my email every ten minutes.	I will set clear times to look at my inbox, for example at 9am, 11:30am, 1pm, 4pm and 6pm. The rest of the time, I will stay logged out of my email.
I never put my phone on silent when I am working.	I will set clear times to check my texts and calls. The rest of the time, I will put my phone in flight mode.

STEP TWO: PLAN THE CHANGE

Your five priority actions

You can use the Eisenhower Matrix to select your five priority actions. This method was inspired by the former US president Dwight D. Eisenhower (1890-1969), who reportedly once said "I have two kinds of problems, the urgent and the important. The urgent are not important, and the important are never urgent". The matrix therefore allows us to classify our tasks based on the criteria of urgency and importance; you will soon see how useful it is to distinguish between the two. The two criteria are represented on the two axes of the following graph: urgency is on the horizontal axis, and importance is on the vertical axis.

The Eisenhower Matrix

Go back to the unsorted list of the things you would like to do but have not got around to and place each of the tasks in one of the boxes of the matrix. Once you have done this, the top left-hand box will be your priority list: it contains everything that is both important and urgent. The good news is that you can abandon all the tasks in the "not important and not urgent" box for good! If all your tasks are in the important and urgent box, start again and think harder about each task to rank them in order of importance and degree of urgency.

You should be left with a short list (no more than five tasks) to carry out quickly. The most decisive stage is done, because you have now precisely defined your objectives. You have gone from "I have so many things to do that I am not doing" to "I have identified five important, urgent tasks that I am going to complete". You have taken a constructive step.

EXAMPLE OF A PRIORITY LIST

1. Organise a meeting with the Dumont Company to review the past year and offer new services for the coming year.
2. Finish my revenue forecast by client and by month.
3. Tidy my desk and throw away or archive half my papers.
4. Set up a meeting with the IT technician to update my computer.
5. Update my CV.

Your time management

Assess how much time you need to carry out each of these actions. If some tasks are too time-consuming, you can break them down into two or three steps. Likewise, if you feel the need, you could try and distinguish the different component parts of a task.

At this stage, it is important to take the time to draw up a realistic "time budget". There is no point artificially inflating the time you need: you will just discourage yourself with the idea of the days of work ahead of you. On the other hand, make sure not to underestimate the scope of the tasks you need to carry out, or you could get a few nasty surprises when you make a start on them. You therefore need to allocate a reasonable amount of time for all the tasks on your list.

Task	Estimated time needed
1. Organise a meeting with the Dumont company to review the past year and offer new services for the coming year.	• Sending a message: three minutes • Preparing for the meeting: three hours
2. Finish the table with revenue by client and by month.	• Two 90-minute sessions
3. Tidy my desk and throw away or archive 50% of papers.	• Two half-days
4. Set up a meeting with the IT technician to update my computer.	• Setting up the meeting: three minutes • Backing up my data: one hour
5. Update my CV.	• Two one-hour sessions

Your planning

Set a deadline for each of your five actions. At this stage, it is also recommended that you take the time to put a realistic plan in place. Give yourself long enough to carry out your tasks so that you do not abruptly switch from procrastination to overactivity. On the other hand, make sure that your plan is stimulating enough to give you a sense of satisfaction in the near future.

It is now time to update our previous list by setting a deadline for each task and sub-task.

Task	Estimated time needed	Deadline
1. Organise a meeting with the Dumont company to review the past year and offer new services for the coming year.	• Sending a message: three minutes • Preparing for the meeting: three hours	• Morning of Monday 4 January • Afternoon of Friday 8 January
2. Finish the table with revenue by client and by month.	• Two 90-minute sessions	• Morning of Tuesday 5 January • Morning of Tuesday 12 January
3. Tidy my desk and throw away or archive 50% of papers.	• Two half-days	• Afternoon of Thursday 7 January • Afternoon of Thursday 14 January
4. Set up a meeting with the IT technician to update my computer.	• Setting up the meeting: three minutes • Backing up my data: one hour	• Morning of Monday 4 January • Morning of Wednesday 6 January
5. Update my CV.	• Two one-hour sessions	• Afternoon of Monday 10 January • Afternoon of Monday 17 January

As you have no doubt noticed, we have put the quickest tasks to carry out first (two telephone calls or emails on Monday morning). Indeed, it can be encouraging to increase your workload gradually. You also need to be able to adapt the tasks to your own way of working. Are you a morning or an evening person? Do you tend to get off to a flying start at the beginning of the week, or do you build up steam as the week progresses? Asking yourself this kind of question can help you to optimise your organisation.

As such, if you are more effective in the mornings, plan the tasks that will require the most energy for that part of the day; conversely, save the tasks that you think will be the least difficult for times when you know you are less productive. Make a note of all the tasks to be carried out in your diary or planner, as you would with meetings, in order to give them the place they deserve in your schedule from now on.

STEP THREE: MEASURE YOUR PROGRESS AND SEE WHAT IS LEFT TO DO

Your evaluation

Once the date of the last deadline arrives, it is the moment of truth: take stock of the situation by drawing up a quantitative and qualitative evaluation of the actions carried out. This simply involves reviewing what you have completely finished, what you have partly finished and what you have not started yet. Go back to your list and evaluate how complete (as a percentage) each task is.

Task	Sub-task	% completed	Number of points
1. Organise a meeting with the Dumont company to review the past year and offer new services for the coming year.	• Sending a message • Preparing for the meeting	100% 70%	1 0.7
2. Finish the table with revenue by client and by month.	• First part • Second part	100% 40%	1 0.4
3. Tidy my desk and throw away or archive 50% of papers.	• First part • Second part	100% Not done	1 0
4. Set up a meeting with the IT technician to update my computer.	• Setting up the meeting • Backing up my data	100% Not done	1 0
5. Update my CV.	• First part • Second part	100% 20%	1 0.2

The last column, "number of points", gives a score quantifying your achievements. To do this, we grant each of the sub-tasks the same degree of importance, even if the time taken to complete them varies considerably. The idea here is to consider that making a quick phone call can be as useful as spending half a day tidying.

In our example, we had five tasks, each divided into two sub-tasks, giving a total of ten points. Taking into account the percentages of completion, we have a score of 6.3 out of 10. How should we interpret this? At this stage, it is essential to adopt a positive outlook on our progress. One approach is to say that we got more than 6 out of 10, meaning more than 3 out of 5 of the tasks we had set ourselves. This is encouraging, but you may think that it is hardly something to celebrate. Another approach is to think that we have gone from 0 out of 10 to 6.3 out of 10 in under two weeks. This is excellent progress, and we can be proud of it. Now is the time to focus on the positive side of this remarkable step forward and savour our victory.

Your analysis

After pausing to appreciate the importance of what you have just accomplished, it is time to take a moment to analyse why some tasks were left unfinished or not even started, in order to understand why you find it difficult to move forward. It is important to tackle this phase calmly and take a step back to focus on the facts. You have made an effort to change, and you need to keep this momentum going. Putting yourself down will not do you any good.

To go back to our example, we need to reflect on why we have partially or completely failed to carry out five of our ten sub-tasks by identifying one or two reasons for each. Some of these reasons may lead us to spot a new urgent task.

Task	% com-pleted	Reason not completed	Action to take
1.Preparation for the meeting with the Dumont company	70%	I do not have all the information on the new projects that the Dumont sales mana-ger presented to my boss a month ago.	Ask my boss to brief me.
2. Second part of the table with revenue by client and by month.	40%	I had underestimated the time needed.	Reschedule two two-hour sessions.
3. Second part of desk tidying.	Not done	No good excuse. I made a good start with the first session, but I let things go with the second one because of tired-ness and a lack of motivation.	Reschedule half a day of tidying (maybe a morning at the start of the week).
4. Backing up the data on my computer.	Not done	I was scared of doing something wrong and losing my data.	Ask a colleague for help.
5. Second part of updating my CV.	20%	On the afternoon of Monday 17 January, I had to cover for a colleague who was ill.	Reschedule a session.

As you will have realised, you need to be honest and accurate. Even if the reason for not carrying out a task is a lack of motivation, as in point 3, the idea is to face up to this reality without beating yourself up and simply reschedule the task. As we have already said, change is a gradual process. You can always try again at something you have not managed so far.

Your next projects

Once you have finished this evaluation, you need to keep your momentum going and continue using the same methods by drawing up a new list of five action items. You can reuse some uncompleted tasks from the previous list, unless new urgent and important priorities have come up since you wrote it. It is best to stick to five tasks.

TOP TIPS

- Look at your difficulties in acting head on, without exaggerating, but also without shying away from them. Carry out a considered evaluation by examining yourself from a distance, as though you were analysing the behaviour of somebody else.
- Focus on the progress you have made rather than on the things you have not managed to do yet. With each accomplishment, look at what you have achieved compared with what you had not achieved previously. Write these accomplishments down on paper if you need to.
- Adopt a policy of small steps. As with going to the gym or running, know how to pace yourself and manage your efforts. Remember: slow and steady wins the race.
- Be aware that the average life expectancy has considerably increased over the last 100 years. Modern humans therefore benefit from an extended temporal perspective. It is important to remember this by knowing how to give ourselves time to alter our behaviour. It is never too late to change.
- Congratulate and reward yourself when you have made progress. Is there a particular concert you have been wanting to go to for a long time? Treat yourself to a ticket when you think you have earned it.
- Do not listen to bad advice. Some people think that they can get rid of their tendency to procrastinate by giving a set amount of money to a friend, on the condition that they will only get it back if they stick to a particular resolution. We do not consider this a valid approach because

it does not involve in-depth reflection.

- Try to ignore negative messages that may have been poisoning your subconscious since childhood. It is not uncommon for us to have been unwittingly conditioned by remarks that have given us a negative image of ourselves: "You will never amount to anything", "You cannot do it", "Hurry up", "Make the adults happy", "Your sister is brilliant, you are not", and so on.
- Do not worry about being a little over-organised. At the start of your process in particular, you may sometimes feel a little obsessive, because your behaviour will completely change. The lists system suddenly turns you into a new person who plans a lot. Embrace this role, have fun with the change in your style and savour the pleasure of your transformation.
- Give yourself some time in the day to take a few deep breaths, empty your mind and really live in the moment.

DID YOU KNOW?

There is an International Procrastination Day every year on 25 March. However, with a bit of work – thanks to our advice – hopefully you will not want to take part in the next one!

FAQS

WHAT EXACTLY DOES THE TERM 'PROCRAS-TINATION' MEAN?

From the Latin *procrastinare*, meaning 'to put off until to-morrow', 'procrastinate' is an increasingly widely-used term which means "keep leaving things you should do until later, often because you do not want to do them" (Collins English Dictionary).

However, procrastinating does not necessarily mean doing nothing, as procrastinators may well accomplish some things while putting off one or more specific tasks for later.

penchant for procrastination in her 1950 novel *En pays connu* ("In a Known Country").

IS THERE A STANDARD PROFILE OF A PROCRASTINATOR?

There is no one standard profile. Ask your friends: it is more than likely that all of them, without exception, procrastinate when it comes to at least one task. According to Piers Steel, an expert in company dynamics and the author of *The Procrastination Equation*, procrastination affects between 15 and 20% of the population.

It is also worth pointing out that teenagers are particularly guilty of procrastination, due to the psychological and hormonal changes that adolescence entails.

OBLOMOVISM

In 1859, the Russian writer Ivan Goncharov (1812-1891) published his novel *Oblomov*, which depicts an apathetic aristocrat named Oblomov (*oblom* is Russian for 'fracture' or 'crack') who spends almost all his time in bed procrastinating. This character became the archetype of the man who is incapable of action, and his name resulted in the coining of the word 'Oblomovism'.

DOES MODERN LIFE ENCOURAGE PROCRASTINATION?

For inhabitants of wealthy countries, physical effort no longer necessarily occupies an obvious central place in modern life. Our ancestors who went out to gather wood could not procrastinate, or they risked dying of cold. Everyday situations in which our lives could be in danger are relatively rare nowadays. It is probably not a coincidence that the word 'procrastination' started to be used more frequently in the 19th century, with the advent of the Industrial Revolution.

At present, in Western societies, it seems to be confirmed that material comfort and immediate access to information may stimulate impulsiveness and laziness. Round-the-clock television and the remote control are not necessarily our best allies in our quest for a sense of effort. How can we develop the desire to act in a society of plenty?

WHAT ARE THE POTENTIAL CAUSES OF PROCRASTINATION?

To go back to the concept of Oblomovism, we can consider that procrastination is linked to a breakdown in the resources that give us the will to act. Although it is difficult to call them causes, some psychological attributes have frequently been linked to procrastination:

- **Anxiety, fear of failure or fear of confrontation with others.** If you do nothing, you cannot fail.
- **Perfectionism.** Some people choose to avoid doing

things rather than risk doing them imperfectly.

- **Low self-esteem.** Not doing things provides some people with confirmation of their belief that they are good for nothing.
- **Impulsiveness.** Some people are only motivated by the prospect of strong emotions. If they are not excited by the idea of spending an afternoon sorting their bills, they are not motivated.
- **The need to be in danger.** For some people, not doing things sometimes puts them in a risky situation, which is a way of feeling intense emotions.
- **Physical and/or mental exhaustion.**
- **Lack of sleep.**
- **An unbalanced diet.**

It is essential to think about which of these characteristics applies to you personally in order to make progress.

THERE MUST BE SOME BENEFITS TO PRO-CRASTINATION. WHAT ARE THEY?

When you let this type of behaviour take hold of you, it is because you get something out of it, in spite of the suffering it causes. We can use the causes of procrastination to deduce its benefits. Procrastination can allow you to:

- avoid facing up to other people;
- maintain a protected, childlike position;
- find reassurance in the fact that you match up to the negative image that adults painted of you when you were a child;

- make yourself seem like someone who is original, out of the ordinary and free from constraints.

You also need to have a serious think about this aspect of procrastination.

WHAT TASKS ENCOURAGE PROCRASTINATION?

The nature and scope of the tasks concerned vary widely depending on the person. An individual may procrastinate at work but be very productive at home, or the other way around. Procrastination may affect one very specific task or area, such as a person's approach to eating ("I'll start my diet tomorrow") or their organisation of their space ("I'll tidy my desk tomorrow", "I'll clean the windows tomorrow"). Finally, a person can be a procrastinator by nature; in this case, they tend to put off all their activities as a matter of course.

HOW LONG WILL IT TAKE ME TO CHANGE MY BEHAVIOUR?

Once you have really decided to change, you can make progress very quickly. You can tackle your plan of action as soon as you have finished reading this guide. Consider that your life is in your hands and it is now up to you to make what you want of it.

I CANNOT MANAGE TO OVERCOME MY PROCRASTINATION ALONE. HOW CAN I GET HELP?

If you have followed our programme to the letter and still cannot carry out at least 40% of the actions you have planned, we strongly recommend that you consult a coach or a therapist. You probably need help from an expert, who will look at your particular case in detail. Know that the decision to seek help is a decisive step in your ability to change your behaviour.

You could also try mindfulness meditation. This may help you to refocus on yourself, concentrate on your aims and relax if you suffer from anxiety.

OVER TO YOU

Below are five very small, easy things to do before tackling your plan of action. They will enable you to embrace the change in you.

- When you get up in the morning, take several deep breaths while raising your hands towards the sky (as you inhale) and gently lowering them (as you exhale).
- For a week, remove one item from your daily diet and replace it with something else. It does not really matter what food you choose; what is important is the process. For example, replace sliced bread with crispbread, coffee with tea, green salad with lamb's lettuce, and so on. If you are not consumed by frustration by the end of the week, keep going with the experiment.
- For a week, change part of your daily routine. Go for a five-minute walk, take a detour, take the bus instead of the underground, etc.
- Every day, write down at least one amusing thing that happened to you during the day. Seeing the funny side of life will give you energy. Reread your notes from time to time.
- When you go to bed at night, take a few moments to visualise a scene in which you are acting with complete calm. Imagine yourself carrying out the first action on your list and watch yourself doing it. The scene should

be very tangible, and you should see it unfolding before
your eyes.

We want to hear from you!
Leave a comment on your online library
and share your favourite books on social media!

FURTHER READING

BIBLIOGRAPHY

- Bandler, R. (1985) *Using Your Brain: For a Change.* Boulder, Colorado: Real People Press.
- *Collins English Dictionary.* [Online]. [Accessed 15 March 2017]. Available from: <https://www.collinsdictionary.com/>
- Perry, J. (2012) *The Art of Procrastination: A Guide to Effective Dawdling, Lollygagging and Postponing.* New York: Workman Publishing Company, Inc.
- Steel, P. (2010) *The Procrastination Equation: How to Stop Putting Things Off and Start Getting Things Done.* Harlow: Pearson Education Limited.
- Thich, Nhât Hanh. (2013) *La plénitude de l'instant. Se réconcilier avec soi-même et avec autrui.* Paris: Poche Marabout.

ADDITIONAL SOURCES

- Allen, D. (2015) *Getting Things Done: The Art of Stress-Free Productivity.* London: Piaktus Books Ltd.
- Burka, J. B. and Yuen, L. M. (2008) *Procrastination: Why You Do It, What To Do About It Now.* Cambridge, Massachusetts: Da Capo Press.
- Duhigg, C. (2013) *The Power of Habit: Why We Do What We Do, and How to Change.* London: Random House Books.
- Fiore, N. (2007) *The Now Habit: A Strategic Program for Overcoming Procrastination and Enjoying Guilt-Free Play.*

London: Penguin.

- Goncharov, I. (2014) *Oblomov*. Trans. Pearl, S. Richmond, Surrey: Alma Classics.
- Pychyl, T.A. (2013) *Solving The Procrastination Puzzle: A Concise Guide to Strategies for Change*. London: Penguin.

50MINUTES.com

IMPROVE YOUR GENERAL KNOWLEDGE

IN A BLINK OF AN EYE !

www.50minutes.com

Made in the USA
Monee, IL
07 July 2026

56545313R00020